A VIEW FROM THE FRONT PEWS

Growing Up in the Family of a Small-Town Pastor

Larry Hoover, Steve Hoover, Tom Hoover,
Kathy Sumner, Linda Barth, Peggy England

Edited by Sara Benner
Cover illustration by Rebecca Douglas
Formatting by Katie Erickson, KatieEricksonEditing.com

ISBN: 9798363791109

Dedication

This book is dedicated to the loving memory of John and Evelyn Hoover.

Dedication

Table of Contents

Table of Contents

Introduction

This document is a tribute to our parents, John and Evelyn Hoover. The remembrances and anecdotes included were provided by all of us who grew up in their family: Larry, Steve, Tom, Kathy, Linda, and Peggy.

Our dad was a pastor in several churches in small towns in Northwest Ohio. He was a pastor from about 1951 to 1991. He served Green Springs EUB Church; Salem EUB/Belle Vernon EUB, near Upper Sandusky; Hoytville EUB; Upper Sandusky Trinity United Methodist; and Delphos Trinity United Methodist. Most of the churches had average morning attendances of less than 200 parishioners, and a couple far less than that. One of the appointments was actually a two-point charge, consisting of two very small churches, Salem EUB and Belle Vernon EUB.

Dad retired from active ministry in 1991, and he and Mom moved into a small retirement home they had purchased in Upper Sandusky. Dad continued to serve as a fill-in pastor for several area churches for several more years, retiring for good in 2010. They eventually moved into an assisted living home, where Mom passed away in 2014 and Dad in 2020.

Remembrances of Larry

Even though Dad started his pastoral career at the Green Springs, Ohio EUB church, I have very few memories of that church, since we moved away when I was about four years old. We moved from Green Springs to the Salem/Belle Vernon two-point charge near Upper Sandusky, Ohio. The parsonage we lived in had a large side yard for baseball and football games, and a barn to play in.

While at that charge, Dad would preach the same sermon at each church every Sunday, once in an early service in one church, and again at a later service at the other church. We kids would attend worship at one church, and then stay for Sunday school while Dad went to the other church.

Dad had opportunities to move to larger churches in larger cities like Lima or Toledo, with larger salaries. That was the typical career trajectory for pastors in the EUB and United Methodist denominations at that time. However, he always declined those moves. He said that there were a lot worse places to raise a family than in small towns like Hoytville or Upper Sandusky.

At every church, we lived in a parsonage provided by the church. (My parents never owned their own home until they retired in 1991.) We had a large family, with three boys followed by three girls, with an age spread of fourteen years from oldest to youngest. Because the parsonages were owned by the church, we had to fit into whatever bedrooms were available in each parsonage. I don't recall any rooms being added to any existing parsonage we lived in to accommodate our large family. That required doubling up, including bunk beds, in many of the parsonages.

There was only one time when we got a new parsonage, when Dad was serving the Trinity UM Church in Upper Sandusky. The old parsonage was a large two-story clapboard house next to the church. For several reasons, the church trustees decided that a new ranch style parsonage should be built in a subdivision away from the church, and the old parsonage torn down for parking. There was a gentleman in the church who built and sold a new ranch style house every year in his part time, and that money funded the college educations of both of his children. This gentleman agreed to supervise the building of the parsonage, and nearly all the labor was donated by church members. By that time, I was out of college and working in Cincinnati, and my two brothers were also in college, I believe. There was an extra bathroom in the basement of the house, and a spare bedroom was constructed down there for whenever any of us came home. I actually got to help with installing the shingles on the house. I came home for the weekend and pitched in with the work on the parsonage. This was probably the closest my parents ever came to having some input into their housing, until they bought their retirement house.

Because our parents were raising six children on the low pastoral salaries that were typical at that time, Dad had to take on odd jobs from time to time. He drove farm trucks, worked at a grain elevator, drove a school bus, raised rabbits, and served as a substitute teacher and a volunteer firefighter to earn extra money.

For many years, Dad was paid from $75 to $90 a week as a pastor, but yet was expected to be on-call 24/7 for the parishioners, and he was always available. Some leaders of these small churches seemed reluctant to pay the full-time pastor more than the lowest amount that any church member made, since many people held the misconception that, "after all, the pastor only works for one day a week."

I recall one situation when two of the church leaders kept Dad cooling his heels upstairs in the parsonage for an hour or more while they were downstairs in the basement discussing whether he should receive a raise of $10 or $20 a week. I always thought that incident was extremely disrespectful to Dad, even though I doubt if I ever heard him complain about it.

Despite the low pastoral salaries, or maybe because of them, most of the churches were generous in other ways. The Hoytville church, for example, always presented us with several bushel baskets full of canned goods, baked items, and other foodstuffs at the conclusion of every Christmas Eve service that was held while we were at that church. My brother recalls the congregation referred to that as "bringing in the sheaves."

Since none of these small churches provided a secretary for Dad, my mom was usually the secretary by default, often without compensation.

She would type Dad's sermons and the Sunday bulletins, print the bulletins off using the mimeograph machine, and sometimes had us kids help fold them. One remembrance I have regarding the sermons is that after Mom typed each week's sermon on Friday or Saturday, Dad would usually practice his sermon in the bathroom on Saturday evening. We could walk past the closed bathroom door and hear him working on the presentation of the sermon. Usually, he added some handwritten notes to the typed text as a result of that practice.

Mom was also pressed into service as the janitor at some of the churches. I believe only at the Upper Sandusky Trinity church was she actually compensated for both her secretarial and janitorial duties, which was a blessing, given the low pastoral salaries mentioned earlier.

Another thing Dad did to support the family was to have a large garden wherever we lived. He would grow peas, green beans, tomatoes, corn, lettuce, radishes, beets, onions, and sometimes more. Whatever we could not eat, Mom would freeze or can it if possible. It was an all-family effort, when it came to planting, weeding, and harvesting the garden produce, as well as freezing or canning. We also harvested non-garden produce, like dandelion greens, and occasionally consumed them. When I got old enough to run the old gas-powered rototiller between the rows of corn or beans, I thought I was big stuff.

When my parents occupied the new Trinity parsonage in Upper Sandusky, their yard adjoined the property of a family in the church. Both Dad and Harold, the neighbor, had gardens that adjoined each other. Dad and Harold were good friends, but there was still a lot of good-natured competition and teasing between them regarding their garden produce. One summer both Dad and Harold had pumpkins planted close to each other in their respective gardens. Apparently, Dad's largest pumpkin was bigger than Harold's for most of the summer, and Dad was giving Harold a hard time about it. When it got close to harvest time, Harold and his son went to a farm they owned near Carey and picked a pumpkin that had been growing there in a former chicken yard that was highly fertilized from the chickens. That pumpkin was huge and was much larger than the one growing in their garden that was being ridiculed (good-naturedly) by Dad. Harold and his son secretly substituted that huge pumpkin for their previous one, overnight, so Dad wouldn't see them make the switch. I understand that when Dad came out to the garden the next day, he was flabbergasted at first by the huge pumpkin that grew overnight. I can only presume that he and Harold had a great laugh over that incident.

My brothers and I all played high school sports, and one side effect of being a PK (preacher's kid) was that the language that some of the coaches used around us was milder than it might otherwise have been, I am sure. I realized later in life that there likely were parties that we were not invited to at that time because of our "PK" stature also. That was undoubtedly a good thing.

Dad played softball for several of the churches he served. Initially, at the Salem church, the team played in a fast-pitch softball league with other church teams. Dad was the pitcher for most of the games. He was essentially a "junk" pitcher, throwing curves, rise balls, and changeups, but not much speed. He later transferred to slow pitch softball and played until he was fifty-eight years old. Dad was well-known for his ability to good-naturedly razz opposing players, what would be called "trash talking" today. One opposing player, who also was a columnist for a local weekly paper, once wrote a column about playing against the Trinity slow pitch team. He said that he felt it was unfair that Trinity's pitcher was a "reverend," because it felt sacrilegious to razz a preacher.

In addition to his other responsibilities, Dad also coached sports. He coached our Little League baseball teams in Hoytville, and my sisters' softball teams in Upper Sandusky.

Dartball was a sport that was and still is popular with small rural churches in several parts of the country. For those unfamiliar with dartball, it is a game played by tossing fat wooden darts with long sharp points underhand at a board that has a baseball diamond painted on it. Areas around the bases were designated as hit areas (singles around first base, doubles around second base, triples around third base, and home runs in a small area in the center of the diamond.) Most of the rest of the board was designated as outs. Each player, when it was their turn, would stand behind a line about 10' from the board and toss the darts one after the other until the player either gets a hit or hits one of the "out" areas. At that point his or her turn ended. The games were scored using a baseball scorebook. In our local church dartball league, the games were held in various church basements around the county. The teams would sit in rows of chairs on either side of the space between the board and the throwing line. This arrangement lent itself to razzing and trash talk between the teams, and Dad was famous (or infamous) for his teasing of the other team's players. Dad was never disrespectful or nasty, and I think some players looked forward to getting razzed by Reverend Hoover. Because Dad was around the area so long, everybody knew him, and every opposing team looked forward to beating his team.

Dad also played golf and taught us boys how to play. Later in life, he always made a big deal (good naturedly) about all the excuses he had before every round of golf: his shoulder hurt, his back was sore, his clubs were crooked, etc. Bob Kane was a good friend of ours who owned a Christian bookstore in Findlay, Ohio, and Dad and I played golf occasionally with Bob and his son, Jim. Bob got to the point where he printed up a list of golf excuses that Dad could hand out before every golf match. He also presented Dad with a coffee mug that was printed with several golf excuses. Bob and Dad had great fun with his golf excuses, but Bob had great respect for Dad. Whenever anyone from Upper Sandusky, where Dad and Mom lived in retirement, bought anything from the Christian bookstore and wanted to pay with a personal check, the first thing Bob asked was whether that person knew John

Hoover, and whether they liked him. If they said yes, no further identification was required: their check was accepted.

We had school teachers in some of these small towns that seemed to take special interest in how we behaved. I remember my fourth-grade teacher at Eden School (near Upper Sandusky) took me aside to lecture me one time about my behavior. Our class had been in line, waiting for something, and I kind of pushed the girl in front of me. This teacher pulled me out of the line, sat me down, and instructed me that since I was a preacher's kid, my behavior should be better than the rest of the kids. I understood that to mean that as PKs our behavior should be held to a higher standard. Ironically, this teacher and her husband are now good friends of my family, and I see them almost every Sunday at church. After that chat from the teacher, I very seldom got in trouble in school from that time on, in contrast with a certain sibling of mine, who shall go unnamed.

In addition to being on good behavior with teachers and other kids, we occasionally were visited by the Conference Superintendent of our denomination. The Conference Superintendent was the person who determined if and when pastoral changes were to be made, so he was essentially Dad's boss. One of these visits stands out for me. The CS had arrived and was waiting for Dad to come home. This particular CS was a serious, strait-laced gentleman, and Mom was probably making small talk while they waited. For some reason my brother Steve and I chose that moment to start being rowdy and bouncing on the couch. Before long, Steve bounced extra hard and put his backside through a window behind the couch. I can only imagine Mom's humiliation and mortification.

One outcome of living in Hoytville was that our house, next to the church, became a hub for activities for the local kids in the community, especially outdoor activities. The church and parsonage were in the center of town, easily reachable with bicycles or on foot. And since it was the preacher's place, with activities organized by the preacher's kids, it was a safe environment.

There was a decent-sized yard between the parsonage and the church, and that area was great for touch football games; baseball and softball pitching practice; setting up tackling dummies for football tackling and blocking practice when we got into junior high football; and wiffle ball games. With some trees down one side of the yard complete with roots above ground, we could set up some very challenging croquet courts as well.

The gravel alley behind the church, which dead-ended into our driveway and our garage, became an Olympic track. We would stretch some twine or a piece of rope across the open garage door, and that was the finish line we would cross, with our arms raised up just like we saw on the Olympic broadcasts on TV. We ran laps around the church and used the yard for field events.

I recall setting up challenging miniature golf courses on our back patio slab, using bricks, drainpipes, tin cans for holes, and scrap lumber to make ramps and rails. I think we became well known around town for our miniature golf courses. One of my classmates, who lived just outside of town, used to tell people that there was always something going on at the Hoover house.

Remembrances of Steve

My time growing up in small towns mostly involved family and/or sports. Being the second oldest in the John and Evelyn Hoover family, I think I was the only of the six kids to have to move twice during my grade school through high school years. I started school going to Eden School (a rural Wyandot County school) for first and second grade. We lived in a parsonage right on old U.S. Route 30, a major east-west cross-country truck route. What I remember about that was to never get too attached to a dog because they always seemed to test the theory that trying to cross a highway like that was easy-peasy. The dog would lose to the semi every time. As I recall, all of the dogs were named Skippy: Skippy 1, Skippy 2, etc., up through at least 6. I do remember, though, Dad rushing out onto the highway in front of an oncoming truck because our neighbor boy from across the highway (about three years old) was trying to cross the highway. Fortunately, that time things ended well.

When we were preparing to make the move to Hoytville (at that time a step up for Dad), one question we wrestled with was "Will I Hoyt myself in Hoytville?" Anyway, the move happened, and we all adjusted to life in a very small town. We pretty much had to create our own fun, and our house was generally the town kids' playground: I remember building many miniature golf courses, using eave spouts, various types of ramps, and spiders and things swinging from trees. One of the neighborhood's favorite games was playing a type of dodgeball in and around the garage—using croquet balls! Then there were the homemade whiffle ball stadiums either at a neighbor house or our house—the right field wall at one of the configurations at our house was the church—no one ever hit a home run over that "wall." As I got closer to junior high age, I spent a lot of time at the tiny local park playing basketball (the only court in town). As I learned, you had to really watch what you said when the games got rough, otherwise the word would come down in a day or two that "that preacher's kid swears a lot." That did not happen during the many times Dad played basketball with us. I know all three of us boys enjoyed the many years Dad spent coaching our little league team—even when he got yelled at by the neighbors for getting their kids' clothes dirty from riding on the drag to get the ball field ready and then not playing them in the game (but they were awful at baseball!)

Who can forget the early family camping trips in a tent when it rained all night? Fun times. The spiritual guidance we received while growing up, however, was next to none, both from Mom and from Dad. One downside: listening to Tennessee Ernie Ford records to wake up every Sunday morning.

Our next move was when I was going into my senior year of high school—to a much larger school, in Upper Sandusky, Ohio, but I adjusted, and life was good. I would not trade my small-town experiences growing up with anyone.

Remembrances of Kathy

My childhood growing up in a large family in a small town was very happy. I don't remember ever feeling unhappy or afraid. As I look back now, while I thought I was just having fun, I was learning some valuable "life lessons."

Most importantly, I learned that a strong faith could help you through the tough times in our lives. This was learned through watching our parents and members of the churches that Dad pastored. I learned that you do what you need to do to provide for your family. Whether that meant taking on side jobs or canning and freezing produce from the garden, or hanging out loads of laundry, you just do, without complaint. This would include the migrant families that would come into our small town each year to help with picking tomatoes, etc.

I learned that people may not be the same behind closed doors. I remember a Sunday school teacher I had that taught us on Sunday, but other days I witnessed her pulling her girls' hair to make them come into the house.

I learned that you could show love to your pastor and others many ways, even if you didn't have a lot of money. I remember people in that church making dresses for my sister and me. I can even remember some of those dresses. They also made Barbie doll clothes. Those were so well made, that I just recently gifted those to my granddaughter!

I learned that family vacations were important to bring family together. Even though staying together in a small camper was challenging, the vacations were forever remembered.

When we moved to a bigger church and bigger school, I learned about "mean girls" firsthand and how to go on after not ever making cheerleader or majorette (unlike my sisters). I went crying to Mom and she said it wouldn't matter in the large scheme of things and she was right.

I learned it was a fine line between wanting to fit in and getting approval from the church family. I was told several times that my skirt was too short.

When I went away to college, I had someone tell me that I was so lucky to be a preacher's kid. And by then, I was able to agree with that. I never really went back to live with Mom and Dad, but it was always "home."

Remembrances of Linda

Although I was born in Upper Sandusky during the time when Dad had the parishes at Salem and Belle Vernon, I was only eighteen months old when we moved to Hoytville, so as the fifth child, that is where my memories begin.

One of my first memories, and definitely when I started realizing that being a PK had its perks, was on my sixth birthday. Baby Peggy decided to make her appearance into the world the day before I turned six. Somehow, several of the church ladies found out that it was my birthday and felt bad that my Mom was in the hospital and unable to bake me a birthday cake. I received six birthday cakes that year!

Another early memory is one Sunday when I walked over to the church all by myself.

The Hoytville parsonage was right beside the church, with just a driveway and large yard separating us. As you can imagine, being the mother of six kids, trying to get everyone out the door and to church on time was quite the task for our poor Mom! I think as long as we were fed and dressed, she scooted us out the door one by one. Well, evidently, one Sunday, she didn't notice that my hair was not brushed. My tight Shirley Temple-like curls must have looked pretty bad. As soon as I walked in the church door, one of the church ladies grabbed me by the arm and shuttled me into the restroom where she attempted for what seemed like hours to get a comb through my tangled mess.

There was a young man in the neighborhood that was known to be quite mischievous. In fact, I believe Mom even referred to him as the town delinquent a time or two. One time it was discovered that someone had put tacks, lots and lots of tacks, on the seats at church. Luckily, they were detected before anyone sat on any. I am not sure if it was confirmed, or just suspected, that the town delinquent was responsible for that little prank! For quite a while after that, I can remember helping to check the church over thoroughly every week.

Another incident I remember was when someone (the town delinquent, perhaps?) was setting fires all over town. I was so scared that our house was going to be next. Mom and Dad assured us that we had enough people in our family to guard all the doors, but I had trouble sleeping for a long time after that.

Our home in Hoytville always seemed to be the gathering place for all the neighborhood kids. Family meals were a top priority for Mom, but evidently, not for some of the other mothers, as there were some of the kids that never needed to be home at a certain time for meals. I remember sitting at the table eating, while some of the other kids, faces pushed up against our screen door, were watching and waiting for us to be done. One particular time, our mild-mannered mother calmly walked over to the door and slammed it shut, right in their shocked little faces.

It was pretty nice growing up in a small town with very little traffic. One of our favorite things to do after a summer rain was to go play in the street. Every puddle was a different room of our make-believe mansion. On the rare occasion a car would come through, we would just step aside and wave to them as they passed by. So when our parents told us to go play in the street, they meant it!

I guess it was the pastor and his family's responsibility to make sure the church was clean and tidy. I can remember spending lots of time at the church with a dust rag in hand, but I am not sure how much help we kids really were because I have more memories of crawling under the pews and running up and down the stairs than I do of dusting! The Hoytville church had classrooms upstairs. There was a staircase that went up both sides, so it was great fun to run up one side and down the other, usually with someone in chase. Also, an empty church made for a great game of hide and seek, another perk of being a PK. I don't think there are very many other kids that have gotten to experience that!

I was too young at the time to understand and appreciate just how dedicated and hard-working our dad was. He was always busy, either with church and meetings, working in his garden or yard, or doing odd jobs. I remember having him as a substitute teacher in my classroom several times and getting to ride the bus when he was filling in as a substitute bus driver. At least once, he taught my class all day and then jumped on the bus to drive a route at the end of the day, and I got to go along!

Mom was also hard-working. She wore many hats as the preacher's wife, but my favorite hat was her Mom Hat! Cooking, laundry, cleaning, helping with homework, and breaking up fights were just some of the daily tasks she tackled as a mother of six! But then there were also all the duties that came with being the pastor's wife, secretary, bookkeeper, confidant, and life partner, in addition to all the committee meetings she was expected to attend. I don't know how she did it, and with such grace and dignity.

In 1969 Dad agreed to a transfer to a larger church in Upper Sandusky. He started at his new parish before school was out, so we had to move out of our house, but wanted to finish the school year out in Hoytville/McComb. So, during the week, Mom and five of us kids (Larry was in college) lived in a camper, parked in a friend's driveway, so we could complete the school year. Moving to Upper Sandusky was a pretty big deal for our family. Although Hoytville was a tiny little village with not a lot to offer, it was all we knew as kids, and we didn't want to leave. To me, as a ten-year-old,

Upper Sandusky was a big scary city. But as it turned out, it was a great little city to grow up in.

Our first parsonage in Upper was just across the driveway from the church. Dad's church office was in the church basement, with a window facing the house. It was pretty handy when we needed to let Dad know dinner was ready, or we needed something. We would just go out and rap on the window. Mom was his secretary and spent a lot of time in that office as well. That window was placed just right that she could keep an eye on the back door of the house while she worked.

We found out quickly that with the parsonage being right beside the church and right on a main state highway, we often had vagabonds, (or "bums," as we so lovingly called them) stop at our house for help. I guess they figured a house so close to a church must be home to some godly people. And they were right, as Dad often gave them money for a meal, gave them a ride somewhere, and even gave them shelter in our camping trailer now and then.

When we moved into the new parsonage, we didn't get those visitors anymore, but Dad still did at the church. And he continued to help them in some way. But Dad reluctantly had to start keeping the church locked because he found some strangers sleeping in the church at times and things were starting to disappear.

We were very fortunate that Dad stayed in Upper to allow all of us to graduate from Upper Sandusky High School, except for Larry, who had graduated from McComb. It wasn't until we were all out of school that he accepted a new charge at Delphos United Methodist. He had opportunities to move to a bigger church with a bigger paycheck, but he always put his family first and didn't want to uproot us.

Remembrances of Peggy

As the youngest of six, and being six years younger than the next in line, my memories are somewhat different than those of my siblings. Being a preacher's kid was never easy, especially when five others had gone before me. Not only did I have to live up to the high standards of being a "PK," but to the high standards my brothers and sisters set. I always felt like I was living under a microscope, because people expected me to be perfect. But that actually was a good thing, as it turned out. I learned to be a good person always—not just when you think someone is watching. It wasn't really the fear of getting in trouble, it was the fear of disappointing Mom and Dad.

All my dad had to do was raise his voice to me to get my attention. I remember a lot of slumber parties when ten little girls would be giggling in the basement in the middle of the night. As soon as my dad would come to the top of the stairs and tell us to settle down, you could hear a pin drop. No one wanted to disappoint my dad.

Being the family of the minister, my sisters and I got loaned out for mother-daughter banquets. Mom had three daughters and she didn't have a selfish bone in her body, so each time there was a mother-daughter event at the church, two of us would go with ladies who were daughterless. We all fought over who got to go with sweet Clara.

When they were getting ready to build the new parsonage, I got to "turn the first dirt" and got my picture on the front page of the Daily Chief-Union, the local newspaper. I felt like a celebrity! That house was the best! I remember watching all the youth group parties of my siblings and trying to memorize all the funny games they played. Then when I was old enough to host, I knew all the tricks!

Life with six kids on a minister's salary was, I am sure, very challenging. But we never seemed to want for anything. We didn't dine out much or go on extravagant vacations. We shared stories around the dinner table and made amazing memories in a tiny camper. I wouldn't have changed a thing.

Remembrances of Tom

Since many of these remembrances that follow are from my childhood, I can't attest that they are 100% accurate. My siblings may remember some things a little bit differently, but this is how the experience of growing up in this wonderful family registered in my memory banks.

We grew up in the era when churches in the Evangelical United Brethren and later United Methodist denominations provided parsonages for pastors and their families to live in. While that system is still largely in place, it is not uncommon today for a pastor to buy his or her own home. As we were growing up, that was almost unheard of. The advantage of the parsonage system was that in the era when most pastors were moved from church to church relatively frequently (every 3-5 years), the pastors were not entangled by having to buy and sell homes frequently. The downside of the parsonage system was that one size did not fit all families, there were often a lot of differences in the quality of housing offered, and providing a parsonage tended to have a negative impact on how much a church would or could pay their pastors. Parsonage living did mean having no mortgage payment, but many small-town pastors arrived at retirement with no equity built up in a home and little savings to secure housing on their own. That scenario definitely played out for our dad and mom.

Our family lived in parsonages our whole lives. We didn't know anything different. Home ownership for each of us kids later in life was a novel experience, as it was for Mom and Dad in retirement. However, even though we always knew the place in which we lived growing up wasn't our *house*, Mom and Dad always did a great job of making sure we always knew it was indeed our *home*.

I was briefly present at Dad's first appointment at Green Springs E.U.B. church. I was only a few months old when Dad received an appointment to a new church. Hopefully there was no connection between my arrival and Dad getting moved. My older brothers, Larry and Steve, had not even started training me in the art of P.K. (Preacher's Kid) mischief at that point. That came later.

Dad's new appointment was to the Salem-Belle Vernon E.U.B. charge, two rural churches east of Upper Sandusky. That's where my first hazy memories of living in a parsonage began. The house was located in the country on Route 30 east of Upper Sandusky. Route 30 was a busy trucking route, and for some reason whenever one of our dogs got loose, they would simply disappear. Apparently, I was spared the gory details at the time of how those two facts were interrelated.

Other than its location, that parsonage had a lot of great features, at least for a little kid. It had a wrap-around porch on which to play that was big enough that I could ride my toy tractor on it. Kathy and I would also fill her toy baby buggy with cats and push them around the porch. Behind the house were all kinds of amusements. There was a swing set and a sandbox made out of a tractor tire where I spent lots of time. There was a long stone driveway that had enough deep depressions in it to make some great mud puddles to play in when it rained. There was also a small barn in the back with a loft in it. I remember gathering up dead grass after Dad mowed the lawn and laboriously hauling it up into that loft where I fashioned it into nests for the chickens. I don't recall that we ever *got* chickens, but I was ready for them in case we did!

In the basement of the parsonage was a huge coal and wood furnace. Dad and one of the farmers in his church would fill the big bin in the basement with wood or coal before winter. I used to be a little intimidated by that big, glowing beast in the wintertime, until I discovered how fun it was to jiggle the big lever on it that shook the ashes to the bottom. Despite its size, it was always quite cold in the winter on the second story of the house where the bedrooms were. After we moved away, someone in the church told Dad that they discovered that the fan blade that was supposed to force air into the second story of the house had been put on backwards. That explained a lot.

A couple hundred yards east of the parsonage there was a "crick" (creek). Years later I went by it and realized it wasn't much more than a drainage ditch, but for me at that time it was a sizeable body of water. One day I decided to go fishing. I grabbed my pole, walked to the crick, dropped my line into the two inches of water flowing by, and waited. Before long Dad appeared in a rather agitated state. It appeared that there was some concern about the fact that I didn't tell anyone where I was going. I really didn't understand what the problem was. I was a confident four- or five-year-old walking alone along a busy trucking highway on the way to a little leisure time. What could go wrong? It didn't turn out well. Dad made me come home, and I didn't catch a thing.

I really didn't understand exactly what Dad did for a living at this point. I just knew we were in one or two churches on a regular basis and Dad was always up there in the front talking.

Belle Vernon was the smaller of the two churches. Dad led worship at both churches every Sunday, but Mom and we kids only went to the Belle Vernon Church occasionally. My only impression of that church was that it was small and there were a lot of older people who sat in the back pews, which meant that Mom and we kids had to sit in pews in front of them. It seemed like every time I looked back at those people, they were staring at us, and most of them weren't smiling.

The Salem church was more fun. I remember coloring with crayons a lot, so I must have been in Sunday school there. There were also more people and they seemed happy and friendly. There were some older girls there that used to sing during church. I had never heard anything like it! They sounded like angels, and they were very pretty. (It mildly disturbs me that I remember the latter impression before age six.) The other fun thing about Salem Church was that the yard around the church had all these cool stones stuck in the ground. They were great for climbing! I had one favorite stone with a rounded top that felt like a saddle. Every Sunday when the weather was nice, I would rush out there after church and ride that pony… until the day that Dad pulled me aside and explained to me that those stones were in fact grave markers, and the people that put them there wouldn't be very happy about me crawling on them. Well, that put an end to a lot of fun, or at least I had to be a little stealthier about it.

I was six years old when Dad was appointed to Hoytville E.U.B. Church in 1960. It became the Hoytville United Methodist Church in 1968 when the Methodist and E.U.B. denominations merged. Although Hoytville was a village of about 250 people, to me it felt like moving to the city! It had all the big city conveniences that I had not experienced before, like sidewalks, streetlights, a post office, and a park. I believe when we first got there, it even had a traffic light! There were also a number of viable businesses in town when we first arrived, including a gas station, a barber shop, a small grocery store, a tavern, a restaurant, a lumber yard, a grain elevator, and a hay mill.

Passing through Hoytville years later, I would think, "How did I ever live nine years in this little place?" At the time, though, it seemed like a great place to grow up. Since we knew everyone in the village and it wasn't that big, we pretty much had the run of the town. We just let Mom know where we were going and off we went, often on our bikes. In the summer we played outside from morning until after dark, ending the day with games of "Hide and Go Seek," "I Spy the Old Gray Wolf," or "Kick the Can." Our home seemed to be a hub for many of those activities. Most of the kids in town seemed to know that's where the action was.

Another reason Hoytville was a great place to grow up is that there wasn't that much around to entertain us, which forced us to get creative at entertaining ourselves. Steve was a master at getting kids together for various sports activities, like baseball, basketball, and football games, as well as his unique creations of a wiffle ball home run derby and homemade miniature golf courses.

The mini-golf enticed some of us to make more of a full-size golf course that ran through the backyards of several of our neighbors. We didn't have any golf clubs, so we hit our golf balls with baseball bats instead. As you might guess, there is an inherent control issue that comes with that arrangement. I found that out the hard way when I teed off and hooked my shot straight through our neighbors' window ten feet to my left. My early golf career ended with me dropping my "club" and running home!

For a while the rage was building wooden race cars using wheels, axels, and wood we scavenged from the town dump. Kids from different families around town would build their own cars and then we would determine a time and street on which to race them. In reality the outcome of the races was much more dependent on the speed of the pushers than the quality of the cars. Regardless, it was rewarding to work with other kids to make something that required a bit of basic design engineering like that. Some good tools skills were also developed in the process.

When we got tired of racing our cars, we turned to demolition derbies instead. Our cars then sported some wicked looking battering rams, which we used to smash each other's cars up until they were inoperable. It was all in fun, though, and we all thought the devastation was hilarious!

Some of our "creativity" was even less well thought out, like the day we decided to play hide and seek on our bicycles using a stop sign as our base. It should come as no surprise that there were some nasty bicycle pileups as contestants raced for the base at the same time, and it was only by the grace of God that there were no severe lacerations from the metal post of the stop sign!

When things got slow in town, there were always lots of country spaces around Hoytville to explore. Creeks were an endless source of fun. We floated objects down the creek and then bombed them with rocks, BB's, or sometimes firecrackers. Creek banks were also great places to build forts and to look for critters. No amount of fancy recreational equipment could ever provide that kind of fun!

Perhaps some of the examples I've shared about our recreational pursuits in Hoytville make it sound more like a spawning ground for little barbarians than a cradle of creativity. It wasn't really that way. We were sometimes ornery (well, my siblings were), but not malicious. You knew everyone in a small town like Hoytville, but that also meant that they knew who your dad and mom were. That was a very potent modifier of behavior! It wasn't the only one, however. Another one was the reason we were there—the church.

The school was an important institution in Hoytville, but Hoytville E.U.B. Church was definitely the heart of the town. In that day the church met both the social and spiritual needs of the community. It was a small but vibrant congregation and was certainly a step up for Dad. For one thing, it gave him the blessing of focusing on one church instead of two. The church had a lot of farm families in it. Usually, several generations of these families attended together. It made for a nice mix of age groups and included a good number of children and youth. Most of the people seemed very friendly and enjoyed each other's company. There were, of course, the usual few grumps and malcontents you find in most churches, just to keep things interesting.

I experienced the church as a modifier of behavior in a positive way and not as a source of judgment. In the back of the church's sanctuary were all the Sunday school classrooms. As I went through grades one through nine living in Hoytville, I can trace in my mind's eye moving through each of those Sunday school classes. Some of the Sunday school teachers I had were more gifted and knowledgeable than others, but somehow God used the good, the bad, and even the deadly boring to begin my spiritual formation. Vacation Bible School was another place where I began to learn both the stories and the lessons of the Bible. It was directed by Dad and held in the Hoytville school for all the kids of the community. Later in my teen years Youth Fellowship was very helpful to me. I think Dad usually directed that as well.

Summer church camp at Camp St. Mary's was another important opportunity the church provided for spiritual growth. Going away for camp for the first time for five days as a fourth grader was hard, but it also provided a great way to get kids out of their normal routines in a fun setting and have some time and special opportunities to think about God. In fourth-grade camp after an evening vesper service, our counselor told us that each of us needed to make a decision about accepting Jesus into our hearts. For some reason, that came as a bit of a shock to me because up to that point I had somehow gotten it into my head that since my dad worked for God, I was automatically in good standing with the Almighty. I would get into heaven on the family plan! This idea that I needed to make my own personal decision about following Jesus had not quite occurred to me. I'm sure that I didn't understand all the theology around what it meant to "accept Jesus into my heart," but I knew I wanted to live for God, so my answer that night was "yes." Two years later at a sixth-grade church camp I felt God's first tugs at my heart about becoming a pastor.

I would like to say that these experiences of spiritual formation at Hoytville Church immediately transformed me into some kind of spiritual giant. Far from it. The spirit may have been willing, but the flesh was weak. Teasing my sisters and arguing with my brothers came a lot more naturally to me than following the teachings of Jesus. I wasn't exactly a spiritual giant at church either. It's hard for a kid to see his dad as Dad the preacher rather than Dad the dad. At least it was for me. It took a long time before I actually began to listen to what my dad was talking about up there from the pulpit. I did discover, however, that if I opened the hymnal and counted the hymns one at a time, Dad was usually done talking before I got to the end. Like I said, not exactly a spiritual giant.

Another example of my spiritual immaturity could be seen in my participation in the church choir. Hoytville Church had a "junior choir" made up of older children that sang in the church services. The director of the choir was a wonderful lady by the name of Grace Long. Participation in this choir was mandatory (per Dad and Mom). I didn't mind singing, and I liked Grace. The problem for me was that choir practice was right after school. For a kid who felt like he had been caged up all day, it was at the worst possible time! I wanted to get outside and play. It just so happened that there was a window at the back of the choir loft, and on warm days it would be open for ventilation. Since there was no screen on the window, it became too tempting for me to occasionally make a quick exit through the window and just hope I wouldn't be missed. It was about an eight-foot drop to the ground from there which stung a bit when I hit the ground, but it seemed worth it at the time.

As far as I know, Grace never snitched on me to my dad, or else I would have heard about it. For reasons I didn't understand, she just kept loving me. Later on, when I became a preacher, I used that story to illustrate God's grace. Not only did I *not* receive the punishment I deserved, I received what I *didn't* deserve—the love and forgiveness of Grace.

At Hoytville I began to understand more of what Dad did, although I realized years later when I became a pastor that I still didn't know the half of it. What I did know was that Dad was gone a lot. I knew absolutely nothing about all the administrative tasks Dad had to do to keep a church going. Only after becoming a pastor myself did I find out what a tremendous amount of time and energy got sucked up by church meetings and denominational meetings. I was oblivious to that when Dad was doing it. I also had no concept of how much time and effort went into preparing a sermon. What all of us kids *did* know was that Dad was in his office a long time on Saturdays and usually worked late into Saturday night, which also meant that our dear mom, his devoted helpmate, was also up late, translating Dad's handwriting which often she alone could decipher and typing up his sermon for the next morning. I always wondered at the time why Dad was often on the couch taking a nap right after Sunday lunch. Years later, I understood.

Dad worked hard at his preaching, but I always thought Dad's real strength as a pastor was relational. He was a shepherd. When people were in the hospital or when tragedy struck, he was there. He also laid the groundwork for good pastoral care by doing a lot of routine calling on his parishioners before they were in crisis, especially the elderly. I always admired the deep relationships he developed with his people in each church he served.

In the process of doing all that calling, though, he would pile loads of miles on his cars. By the time he would get one car paid off, it would be worn out and he'd have to look for another one. I don't think I remember a time growing up when a car payment wasn't a significant part of the family budget, and that was long before churches began reimbursing pastors for the business use of their cars.

I never had the feeling growing up that we were poor, but I was aware that money was always very tight. We lived modestly, but there were always bills that Dad and Mom were paying on but only rarely or slowly paying off. It seemed that there was usually too much month left at the end of the money. Often the moment Dad's paycheck was dropped off we made a very quick trip to North Baltimore to the bank and grocery store.

Since Dad used so much gasoline in his work, he started having it delivered in bulk because it was cheaper than buying it at a gas station. We had a big steel gasoline tank that was elevated on a metal frame. I remember on a number of occasions my brothers and I helping to tip the tank to get the last drops out of it because we had no money for a new delivery. For a while we were getting an "allowance" of twenty-five cents a week, but when school was in session it wasn't uncommon for Mom to have to borrow that quarter back for lunch money or milk money before the end of the week.

Mom and Dad worked very hard at making sure the tight money didn't mean skimping on nutrition. Dad was a prolific gardener. At one time he had three sizeable gardens going—one in our backyard and two at other people's homes who let him use their garden plots. All the produce that wasn't eaten fresh was canned, frozen, or pickled by Mom, which was a huge endeavor while she also tended to us six kids. She also canned peaches and pears that we bought in bulk. Mom was also very creative at stretching our food dollars. We ate a lot of casseroles. I remember there was also a period of time when, except for perhaps baloney sandwiches at lunch, meat was pretty much a delicacy reserved for Sunday dinner only. I don't think that austerity lasted a long time, but whatever the situation was that caused it, we were never wanting for food. It just wasn't always the food that we necessarily preferred to eat.

Dad also tried to help the money situation by taking on extra work opportunities, like substitute teaching, school bus driving, driving truck for area farmers during harvest, and selling cleaning products. I'm sure that added a lot of stress to getting his church work done, but I don't remember ever hearing him complain.

The tight family finances did have a positive impact on us kids in some ways. As soon as we were old enough, we pitched in with the garden work and the canning and freezing of produce. It made us all feel like we had a part in providing food for the family. We boys were also motivated to earn our own spending money. We mowed lawns for older people around town and eventually worked for area farmers baling hay and straw or hoeing soybeans. Larry and Steve also detasselled corn for the DeKalb seed corn company for a few summers. It definitely helped us develop a good work ethic.

I don't remember anyone in the Hoytville community being affluent, so I'm sure we weren't the only family in town who had to pinch our pennies. I do remember one especially kind gesture by the people of Hoytville Church in the days leading up to Christmas. We were having an evening service at the church and at the end they asked our family to come to the front of the church. The person in charge said they had a surprise for us. With that, the pianist started playing and everyone started singing the hymn, "Bringing in the sheaves, bringing in the sheaves, we shall come rejoicing bringing in the sheaves…" All of a sudden, in the back of the church this long line of men came strolling down the aisle and each one had a big bag of groceries in each arm which they proceeded to set on the front pew of the church. When the song was over, the lady said it was all for us—a Christmas present! I had never seen so much food in one place in my whole life! It was so kind. The Hoovers were living large for at least the next month!

The threat of "moving" was always a dark cloud that hung over a pastor's family. Pastors in the E.U.B. and United Methodist Church agreed to be "itinerant" as part of their ordination vows, meaning they had to be willing to move to a new appointment when their bishop said so. We were blessed that our dad tended to stay longer at his appointments than most pastors. While we were at Hoytville, Dad was being considered for an appointment to a church in Toledo. We actually took a drive up there to see the parsonage, and we kids were mortified by what we saw! The houses were really close together, there was almost no yard space, and the area just looked scary. I don't remember how much whining and complaining we did on the way home. It must have been a lot because Dad somehow got out of being considered for that appointment, even though it would have been a bigger church for him. I don't think that was the only time Dad turned down an advancement in consideration of us.

The day came, though, when the dreaded move happened. I still remember the moment I found out. I was a freshman. Steve and I were both participating in track at McComb High School at the time and had just jogged the six miles home from McComb after track practice. (It must have been a sibling challenge.) Steve and I were eating a late dinner when Dad told us we were moving to Upper Sandusky. I thought my world was coming to an end. I remember being so angry that I had no say in the matter, and I immediately began grieving over everything I would lose—friends, a girlfriend, sports, everything familiar. Dad's appointment started at Upper Sandusky Trinity U.M. Church in April. Fortunately, we were at least able to finish the school year out at McComb School by living with Mom during the week in our camping trailer that Wes and Grace Long let us park next to their house.

In the end, my life didn't come to an end. Trinity UMC was a really good and well-deserved advancement for Dad, and at Upper Sandusky High School I made many new friendships that I still cherish today, had new sports opportunities, and, yes, even found new girlfriends. My sisters Kathy, Linda, and Peg all did at least half their schooling there and thrived. Linda and Peg ended up settling there after marrying Mike and Dean, respectively, both Upper Sandusky men. Larry was already in college at Ohio Northern on his way to becoming a civil engineer, so the move did not seem to affect him that much. I always felt bad for Steve, though, because he got caught in that move between his junior and senior year in High School. At McComb he was the starting quarterback on the football team and a starting guard on the varsity basketball team. He still did well at sports at Upper Sandusky, but that school was three or more times larger than McComb and it was hard to break into the same positions he had played as a senior. Still, he persevered, made new friends, and eventually married Diana, an Upper Sandusky bride, and set up a very successful dental practice in Upper Sandusky.

Upper Sandusky Trinity didn't quite have the same "small-town" feel as Hoytville Church, but it was a good church. I grew quite a bit there. They had a really good high school Sunday school class and an active youth fellowship group that went on a very impactful mission trip while I was there. I also got involved with the Fellowship of Christian Athletes group at the high school, which helped me combine my faith and my love of sports and make more sense of both. After graduation, I went on to Otterbein College, on to seminary, and on to marriage to Gretchen and my first appointment in ministry while Dad was still at Trinity UMC.

Over my lifetime, I have met quite a few fellow PK's. A solid majority of them seem somewhat scarred by the experience. In fact, I spoke to a high school PK classmate recently who said she made her fiancé swear that he had no interest in ever going into the ministry. Another said he could never get over the fact that his dad was a different person in the church than he was at home.

I never felt that being a PK was a burden. In fact, I always felt proud to be a PK because I always felt like Dad's main job was to help people, and that was a good thing. I never thought Dad and Mom laid a guilt trip on us to "be good" because we were PK's. They wanted us to be good because that was the right way to live. It was what Jesus taught us to do, and that didn't just apply to PK's.

The other thing that made being a PK feel easy is that Dad and Mom were the same people at home as they were in public. They were both very genuine. Sure, everyone "lets their hair down" at home a bit (not literally for Dad, who was bald). Dad would sometimes get upset with parishioners or issues in the church and vent a little at home—not at us, but just at a situation. I for one appreciated him modeling that kind of honesty instead of acting like everything was always hunky dory. I remember him declaring one evening at the dinner table, "There are more nuts per square inch in this town than anywhere on earth!" I don't remember what brought that statement on, but it showed me that even grown-ups that I respected sometimes get frustrated by others and home is a safe place to share that with people who love you.

Dad always liked to joke and laugh with people in public, but at home he could also be downright goofy. We used to beg him to watch Bugs Bunny with us on Saturday mornings just because we loved to listen to him laugh at the cartoons! Dad was also big on making grand entrances. He and Mom had this routine where he would come through the door, strike a pose, and say, "Lover, it is I!" To which Mom, feigning disinterest, would reply, "Sheesh!" Or sometimes he would bust out in his best operatic voice, "O sole mio…" To which we kids eventually learned to reply, "I'll sella you-oh…" And he would laugh.

After Mom and later Dad died, I think all of us kids felt a deep sense of gratitude for the blessings we received from "Growing Up in the Family of a Small-Town Pastor." Their care, guidance, and love set us off in a good direction. I look at each of my siblings today and see the fabric of Dad and Mom's lives woven into their lives as well as my own. We all love our families with the same intense devotion with which we were loved. And I never DREAMED I would be saying this as one of six screaming, scrapping kids growing up in the parsonage, but I actually love each one of them!

God's love.

Family love.

That's our heritage, and it makes us rich beyond measure.

www.ingramcontent.com/pod-product-compliance
Lightning Source LLC
LaVergne TN
LVHW010504160826
845677LV00012B/2643

* 9 7 9 8 3 6 3 7 9 1 1 0 9 *